THE LIGHT-HEARTED BIBLE STUDY™ SERIES

Overcoming
DIFFICULTIES

A light-hearted look at Joshua

Marilyn Meberg

THOMAS NELSON PUBLISHERS®
Nashville

THE LIGHT-HEARTED BIBLE STUDY™ SERIES

OVERCOMING DIFFICULTIES

A LIGHT-HEARTED LOOK AT JOSHUA

MARILYN MEBERG

THOMAS NELSON PUBLISHERS®

Nashville

Transcribed and compiled by Alice Sullivan

Published by Thomas Nelson, Inc.
P.O. Box 141000
Nashville, TN 37214

Unless otherwise indicated, all Scripture quotations are from *The Holy Bible*, New King James Version (NKJV). Copyright 1979, 1980, 1982 by Thomas Nelson, Inc. Used by permission. All rights reserved.

Scripture quotations marked (NCV) are taken from *The Holy Bible*: New Century Version (NCV). Copyright © 1987, 1988, 1991 by W Publishing Group, a Division of Thomas Nelson, Inc. Used by permission. All rights reserved.

Library of Congress Cataloging-in-Publication Data is available.

ISBN 0-7852-5242-8

Printed in United States

03 04 05 06 07 – 5 4 3 2 1

FOREWORD

Spend five minutes with Marilyn Meberg, and you'll learn three things about her: She loves life. She loves her family. And she loves God.

As a core speaker for Women of Faith, she has shared her personal testimony of heart-wrenching loss and abiding faith with more than two million women. Her love for life is demonstrated over and over in her outrageously colorful and poignant stories. No life lesson escapes Marilyn's eye. She manages to find God's heart and funny bone in every one of life's topsy-turvy turns.

Marilyn frequently and affectionately mentions her family in books and onstage. Her dear husband and comedic partner, Ken, died thirteen years ago of pancreatic cancer, but he is alive and well in the chronicles she shares about their life together. Her grown children, Jeff and Beth, also make regular appearances in her stories, as do her darling grandchildren, Alec and Ian.

Listening to Marilyn talk about the Bible is invigorating. Her love for God makes the Bible palpable and enjoyable for every gender, race, age, and denomination. If you witness her onstage or read any of her books, you know she has a masterful grasp of the Bible and she's a woman after God's own heart.

She is the multitalented, marvelous, magnetic, mirthful, madcap Marilyn Meberg.

Marilyn Meberg is the author of several books, including *The Zippered Heart, Choosing the Amusing, The Decision of a Lifetime, I'd Rather Be Laughing*, and *Assurance of a Lifetime*. She is also a contributor to *The Great Adventure Devotional, Living in Jesus* (a Women of Faith study guide), *Women of Faith New Testament with Psalms and Proverbs*, and the *Women of Faith Devotional Bible*.

CONTENTS

CHAPTER 1

GOD'S CONTINUAL PRESENCE

On my 40th birthday, my late husband, Ken, and I went out for dinner and we decided, at this stage in our lives, we would make a list of those things we wanted to do before we felt we were too old to do them. We each scribbled our list on napkins, and one of the things I scribbled was "skiing." I had never been on skis and was dying to go because I love speed. We prioritized and compared our lists. Skiing wasn't on Ken's list, but river rafting was on his list. We agreed I would go river rafting with him, and he would go skiing with me.

That was in April. Two weeks later, there were wonderful sales on ski clothes, so I bought a whole outfit at half price and brought it home to show Ken. Eight years later, on a New Year's Eve, some very persistent friends coerced him into signing an agreement stating we would go skiing with them in March.

In February, Ken began complaining and coming up with reasons why it would be impossible for us to keep our ski date. But I would not relent. The night before we were to leave, Ken did what he often did when he didn't want to do something: He began to gather together a cold. The afternoon before we were to leave, he called me from the office with a sore throat. Several hours later, he called me sniffing. The next morning, we got into the car, and Ken was blowing his nose and carrying on like his head would fall off.

God reminded Abraham,

*"Little by little I will drive them out from before
you, until you have increased, and you inherit
the land."* (Ex. 23:30)

We got to the condo (which was gorgeous), and it was the perfect
setting for a day on the slopes. We had rented skis, and I watched
with excitement as people walked down the snow-packed road with
their skis slung over their shoulders. We put on our ski boots, which
felt like they were made of cast iron. I couldn't get my feet to bend!
It was like being in rehab. Meanwhile, Ken was still blowing his nose
and sniffing.

We decided to get individual lessons for just the two of us with
an instructor named Kathy. She explained to Ken how to "snow
plow" and how to walk up a slope by turning the skis sideways. I
thought, *Piece of cake.* So, Ken went up the little slope and came down
and stopped. With extreme difficulty, I crossed my skis and put one
on top of the other. I finally made it up the slope, turned my skis,
and came down. Suddenly Kathy yelled, "Snow plow!" I crossed my
skis instead. Ken, who was suddenly an expert after only one lesson,

began yelling instructions to me. I wanted to tell him to just blow his nose.

We moved on to the lift, which led to the beginner slopes. The lift was engaged by hanging on to a rope.

When the rope came toward me, it went right over the top of my head.

Kathy, who stood beside me, grabbed the rope and said, "Get on!"

I dropped my poles.

She ran alongside me and told me to put the poles under my arm, so I did.

But I let go of the rope.

The lift moved on and I was left in the snow. Ski expert, Ken, who had already gone up the lift and come back down, began to give me instructions again. Needless to say, I was not happy. The snow was everywhere and my glasses were fogged. But Ken was no longer sniffing. In fact, he felt great.

I felt a sore throat coming on.

VERSED IN VICTORY

I had an expectation that wasn't met. I found myself riddled with inadequacies, with no apparent cure, and I found myself waiting for the fruition of my dream. In the Book of Joshua, the children of Israel experienced many of the same feelings of lost expectations while waiting to claim the Promised Land.

While examining how God dealt with Joshua the man—with his feelings of inadequacy, his dreams, and his fears, we also see how God's continual presence is working through His promises to us. But first, we have to go back to the beginning—to the Old Testament. In Genesis 12:1, 2, God appeared to Abraham and said,

> *"Get out of your country, from your family and from*
> *your father's house, to a land that I will show you. I will*
> *make you a great nation;"*

The first promise made to Abraham was that he and his family would be directed to a new land. And on that land God promised to create a great lineage through Abraham. In Genesis 13:15, 16, God said to Abraham,

> *"...for all the land which you see I give to you*
> *and your descendants forever. And I will make your*
> *descendants as the dust of the earth; so that if a man*
> *could number the dust of the earth, then your descendants*
> *also could be numbered."*

What was so colossal about this promise from God? Well, Abraham had no children! How strange for God to tell him, "All your descendants as numerous as the grains of sand, you see in front of you." Abraham didn't exactly express a lack of faith, but in the fifteenth chapter he reminded God that he still didn't have any descendants. Abraham asked in jest if the man living in his house would become his heir. To that, God replied,

> "'This one shall not be your heir, but one who will come from your own body shall be your heir. Then He brought him outside and said, 'Look now toward heaven, and count the stars if you are able to number them.' And He said to him, 'So shall your descendants be.'" (Gen. 15:4, 5)

God is very visual, you see. He is very concrete. So He reminded Abraham, "If you can count the stars, you can count your descendants. If you can count the grains of sand on the earth, you can count your descendants." Once again, Abraham didn't have a descendant! Then God prophesied to Abraham regarding the Egyptian captivity. God said,

> "'Know certainly that your descendants will be strangers in a land that is not theirs, and will serve them, and they will afflict them four hundred years. And also the nation whom they serve I will judge; afterward they shall come out with great possessions.'" (Gen. 15:13–15)

CROSSING THE JORDAN

Those were amazing promises God made to Abraham. He called him forth and said to him, "You will have so many descendants you can't count them! However, in the process of getting the land I'm promising you, you will have 400 years of captivity. But I'll bring you out, and then you'll possess the land." God laid out the plan for Abraham, and Abraham believed Him—until, of course, God took too long.

SEARCHING THE HORIZON

1. The Bible is chock full of stories about impatient characters. It seems natural for us to become impatient when we have to wait. Proverbs 13:12 tells us what happens when our desire is fulfilled. Read that verse and write down what you think it means.

a longing fulfilled is the tree of life.

_____

_____

_____

_____

_____

_____

_____

_____

_____

_____

2. What do you do when you think God is taking too long to answer your prayers? Check all that apply.

☑ I pray more.

☑ I take matters into my own hands.

☐ I refuse to pray anymore until God answers my prayers.

☑ I try to be still and listen to what God is telling me about what I want.

☐ _____

VERSED IN VICTORY

When we take matters in our own hands, God makes alternative plans. But we can still manage to mess things up! Abraham had his first child, Ishmael, by his bondwoman, Hagar. That was not God's plan, but God, in His graciousness, still made good on His promise. Then, Abraham had a son, Isaac, with his wife, Sarah. The lineage of Ishmael became the Arab nations, and the lineage of Isaac became the Jewish nation. God said there would be strife between the lines of Ishmael and Isaac. However, from Isaac's line came Joseph, who went to Egypt and eventually gave birth to the Hebrew nation.

Moses was designated to take the children of Israel out of Egypt. But Moses died, and Joshua was appointed to take them farther into the Promised Land.

CROSSING THE JORDAN

Let's get back to God's statement, "Little by little, I will drive them out, and the land will be yours." This is a scriptural principle that applies to us today.

God always makes good on His promises. And almost always, He does it little by little.

I have a confession to make. I want it to happen fast! I like speed! I don't want to wait! For me, if I don't get instant gratification—if I don't get instant promise in my life—something happens inside of me. So I pray more, I learn more about trusting, I learn more about waiting and believing and patience—all of which I have very little.

SEARCHING THE HORIZON

1. Match up the following verses with what the Bible says about patience.

_c_ Psalm 37:5   a. If it concerns me, God will perfect it.

_a_ Psalm 138:8   b. It is better to be patient than proud.

_d_ Lamentations 3:26   c. God brings His will to pass if I trust in Him.

_b_ Ecclesiastes 7:8   d. It is good to hope and wait quietly for God's salvation.

A TIME TO PRAY

Heavenly Father, I know that I am fearfully and wonderfully made, but sometimes I wonder why You also made me so impatient! Every time I want something and I ask for Your help in getting it, I grow tired of waiting, and I admit that a small part of me loses faith in Your ability to help me. Lord, please forgive me. Forgive my impatience and lack of faith. Help me to trust in Your ways and in Your time. With each day that passes, help me see that my impatience is just one more way You are trying to draw me nearer to You. In Christ's name, Amen.

CHAPTER 2

GOD UNDERSTANDS OUR HUMANITY

In Isaiah 40:31, we are given a promise:

*"But the people who trust the LORD will become
strong again. They will rise up as an eagle in the sky;
they will run and not need rest; they will walk
and not become tired."* (NCV)

God uses earthly things to make His principles clear. Did you know an eagle cannot fly using its own power? If an eagle were on your patio flapping its wings, it couldn't become airborne. A bird that big is powerless unless it is sitting high on a mountain or a tree with its wings spread. It waits for a gust of wind to catch it, and then it flies.

God says you and I are like eagles. When He sends the wind, we will rise like eagles and we will be victorious, little by little. You may be a patio flapper, but you won't get anywhere. Personally, I don't like waiting, but that's God's principle.

VERSED IN VICTORY

Now let's talk about Joshua the man—the emotions he felt with the "little by little" concept, as well as the emotions he felt about assuming leadership from Moses. Joshua was a military man, hand-picked by both God and Moses. He was even a priest to Moses. You can imagine what qualities Joshua would have possessed with that kind of expertise, but the first chapter gives us a picture of him that doesn't seem to fit.

Joshua was scared about taking charge after the death of Moses. We know this because God kept saying to Joshua, "Be courageous." He was suddenly in charge of two million people who tended to be a bit temperamental and complained a lot. There were times they even wanted to kill Moses because things weren't happening the way they wanted. So naturally, Joshua was a little frightened.

CROSSING THE JORDAN

Take a moment to zero in on one battle that presently exists in your world—a pain, a hurt, or a tension that needs resolving. Like Joshua, God can say to you, "Be of good courage, I will never leave

Many years ago, we lost a baby girl. She was only 15 days old. To this day, I feel a bond with women who have lost a baby. That woman knows my experience. I know her experience. I've been there. Scripture says Jesus has been there, too. He knows what you feel. If you are divorced and you know others in the Christian world who are divorced, you know the bond that grows when you talk to a woman whose husband left after 20 years of marriage. Through the sharing of the pain, the shock, and the rejection, you experience a bond. Scripture says Jesus did that, too. He has been where you and I have been, and because He's been there, He doesn't judge us in our weakness. He doesn't judge us when we're afraid. Instead, Scripture tells us to "... come boldly to the throne of grace, that we may obtain mercy and find grace to help in time of need." (Heb. 4:16)

you or forsake you." If you have a battle, you can relinquish it to God. After all, it's His battle. And it's already won.

SEARCHING THE HORIZON

1. According to 2 Timothy 1:7, what has God given us instead of a spirit of fear?

2. We all lack courage at times. Do you remember a time when you were afraid of doing something? Was it at a recital, a haunted house, or making a speech in front of people? Write down your most terrifying experience.

_____

_____

_____

_____

_____

_____

_____

_____

_____

_____

_____

_____

_____

3. Try to imagine the worst thing you could go through in life. What would that experience look like?

_____

_____

_____

_____

_____

_____

_____

_____

_____

_____

_____

_____

_____

_____

Now ask yourself, "Who goes before me in battle? Who is my Armor and my Shield? Who already wins the battle for me?"

A Time to Pray

Father, You know my heart. There isn't a day that passes when my battles are not known in every detail by You. There is not a painful or a sore place that You don't long to heal and bring wholeness. Lord Jesus, enable me to allow You to completely envelop me and completely invade my being. Bring healing, bring victory, and bring faith to me. Help me to believe that I can let go of that battle, knowing it's not mine anyway. Thank You for Your love, and thank You for Your consistent presence. In Jesus' name, Amen.

NOTES

CHAPTER 3

God Gives Us the Plan

When I was engaged to Ken, I was somewhat hesitant because I didn't feel I had gotten everything out of my system. After all, I was only 19, and we were to be married when I was 21. You see, I wanted a Fiat convertible. Upon graduation from college, Plan A was to marry Ken. Plan B was to get a Fiat convertible and move to California.

I was attending college in Washington at the time, and it rained constantly, which I hated. You can't get a suntan there! You mildew or you rust. I'm a California woman! I wanted a convertible, and I wanted to drive through the beach cities in California with my hair waving behind my Fiat. But Plan A prevailed and I married Ken. After many years of marriage, he did the sweetest thing. He bought me a Fiat convertible.

Versed in Victory

Let's take a look at the second chapter of Joshua, where we find this fabulous story about a woman named Rahab. To refresh our minds, let's read verses 1–21:

> *Now Joshua the son of Nun sent out two men from Acacia*
> *Grove to spy secretly, saying, "Go, view the land, especially*

Jericho." So they went, and came to the house of a harlot named Rahab, and lodged there. And it was told the king of Jericho, saying, "Behold, men have come here tonight from the children of Israel to search out the country." So the king of Jericho sent to Rahab, saying, "Bring out the men who have come to you, who have entered your house, for they have come to search out all the country." Then the woman took the two men and hid them. So she said, "Yes, the men came to me, but I did not know where they were from. And it happened as the gate was being shut, when it was dark, that the men went out. Where the men went I do not know; pursue them quickly, for you may overtake them." (But she had brought them up to the roof and hidden them with the stalks of flax, which she had laid in order on the roof.) Then the men pursued them by the road to the Jordan, to the fords. And as soon as those who pursued them had gone out, they shut the gate. Now before they lay down, she came up to them on the roof, and said to the men: "I know that the LORD has given you the land, that the terror of you has fallen on us, and that all the inhabitants of the land are fainthearted because of you. For we have heard how the LORD dried up the water of the Red Sea for you when you came out of Egypt, and what you did to the two kings of the Amorites who were on the other side of the Jordan, Sihon and Og, whom you utterly destroyed. And as soon as we heard these things, our hearts melted; neither did there remain any more courage in anyone because of you, for the LORD your God, He is God in heaven above and on earth beneath. Now therefore, I beg you, swear to me by the LORD, since I have shown you kindness, that you also will show kind-

ness to my father's house, and give me a true token, and
spare my father, my mother, my brothers, my sisters, and
all that they have, and deliver our lives from death." So
the men answered her, "Our lives for yours, if none of you
tell this business of ours. And it shall be, when the LORD
has given us the land, that we will deal kindly and truly
with you." Then she let them down by a rope through the
window, for her house was on the city wall; she dwelt on
the wall. And she said to them, "Get to the mountain, lest
the pursuers meet you. Hide there three days, until the
pursuers have returned. Afterward you may go your way."
So the men said to her: "We will be blameless of this oath
of yours which you have made us swear, unless, when we
come into the land, you bind this line of scarlet cord in
the window through which you let us down, and unless
you bring your father, your mother, your brothers, and all
your father's household to your own home. So it shall be
that whoever goes outside the doors of your house into the
street, his blood shall be on his own head, and we will be
guiltless. And whoever is with you in the house, his blood
shall be on our head if a hand is laid on him. And if you
tell this business of ours, then we will be free from your
oath which you made us swear." Then she said, "According
to your words, so be it." And she sent them away, and they
departed. And she bound the scarlet cord in the window.

CROSSING THE JORDAN

This is a thrilling account on so many levels. Several years have transpired since God made the promise to Abraham. And now, the children of Israel were camped on the other side of the Jordan River looking over at Jericho, the first city of the Promised Land.

Joshua sent spies over to check it out. But why did Joshua send spies if the battle was already won?

First of all, on the human level, Joshua was a military man. He was trained in thinking ahead of the enemy and planning what seemed most expedient. So it was within his nature, training, and inclination to send spies, just to see what he was up against in case of a battle. God had already promised this land to the children of Israel, but Joshua did what seemed best and wise according to his training.

What also stands out about this story is what God did for Rahab. God knew this woman was ripe for salvation. In all the wickedness, idolatry, and sinfulness for which Jericho was known, she stood out because she had a budding faith. God honored that faith. He halted the progress of two million people, in the completion of an incredibly long plan, for one woman.

God is like that, though. He is a God of individuals. One person, as well as the masses, is always of tremendous interest to God. God ordained spies to be sent to Jericho because there was a woman there

Someone once asked me very tactfully, "How does it happen that you taught English and then became a shrink and now you're teaching the Bible?" I don't have a clue! Before I taught English at Biola University in California, I taught Women's Bible studies for several years and I loved it. If I had it to do over in this era, I'd love to go into ministry. I love to preach, I love to counsel, and I love people.

whom God wanted to save. It's interesting that these men, thinking they were just doing their duty by going into Jericho, met the one woman in town—a complete stranger to them—who was there to save, protect, and hide them.

God orders your steps, as well. He invites you to be a part of the process, but He is ultimately in charge. God, in His graciousness, invites our participation in the process of His plan. That is very gracious, don't you think? In unity and oneness with God, He allows us to be a part of the process for a battle that has already been won! We aren't just robots, manipulated by a sovereign God. We are His creation, directed by a loving God.

Searching the Horizon

1. God works in us to do His good pleasure. What part do we play in God's plan, according to the following verses?

Philippians 2:13

we are a tool & an instrument

Psalm 37:23

If we are following God's will, obedient, He will direct our path & will bless us accordingly.

2. Think of the times God has worked through you to help others. What were those instances and how did you feel?

It is better to give than receive

A TIME TO PRAY

Lord, what is Your one plan for me? Am I the one You want to save? I can certainly manage to find myself in situations where I need to be rescued. Why is that? Could it be Your way of getting my attention? Father, I want to be more like Joshua. Please give me the wisdom to think ahead by sending You as my emissary into every situation, to be my eyes and ears, and to guide me in my decisions. In Jesus' name, Amen.

CHAPTER 4

A GOD OF INDIVIDUALS

When I was teaching at Biola University, I had to get the syllabuses for the new semester on the secretary's desk by Saturday before Monday classes began. My daughter, Beth, who was 16 at the time, decided to go with me on my little errand. When I got there, I discovered the doors were locked. I knew I would have to go all the way over to the administration building, get a pass key, leave my driver's license, and go all the way back to my building. It was a hassle but I did it.

I put the syllabuses on the desk, and when I left my building, I thought, *Rats, I have to walk all the way back over to the other building to give them this key and then go back to the car!*

Remember the little Fiat Ken gave me? That's what I was driving. As I looked over at the administration building, I thought, *I wonder if my Fiat would fit on these little sidewalks?* You see, one of the fun things about my car was that it would go anywhere. And when you were done, you could put it in your purse!

The semester was finished, everybody had gone away for the weekend, and there appeared to be no one in sight. So I said, "Beth, I have to return this key. But we're in a hurry, so I'm going to drive on the sidewalk." She was justifiably horrified! At 16, she did not appreciate some of my moments.

"God even knows how many hairs are on your head." (Matt. 10:30, NCV).

The sidewalk to the building was a straight shot except for a rose garden in the middle of the path. I lined up my car, made sure no one was around, and headed down the sidewalk. I came to the roses and navigated them beautifully, thank you very much. The tires fit perfectly on the sidewalk.

Suddenly, I heard honking. I looked in my side mirror and saw a Biola security squad car parked at the entrance to the sidewalk. I thought, *Why stop now?*

The squad car then began to pursue me! I saw him get on the sidewalk, and to my gratification, his tires hung off either side. When he came to the roses, he swung wide into the grass. About the time he turned on the siren, Beth sunk to the floorboards.

Since he seemed to be a little bit anxious, I decided I would stop. After all, I didn't want to acquire the reputation of being a fugitive of the law. I got out of my car and went around to meet him at our bumpers. He stood staring at me, and sputtered, "Where are you going? What are you doing? Did you hear me honk? Did you notice the siren?" He seemed a bit agitated. Imagine that!

Now you see, with each of his questions I drew a blank. I didn't know why I was doing what I was doing, and I didn't know how to explain it to him. So, I said, "I don't know if you'll be able to understand this, but I'm in midlife crisis. I get these urges. I don't know where they come from. This was one of them."

He said, "Well, where were you going?"

"I was just going over to the administration building to pick up my driver's license."

After a moment, he said, "I'm not going to give you a citation. However, I am going to ask you to turn around and go all the way back to the parking lot and walk over to get your driver's license."

So while I could turn around on the sidewalk, he could not. He had to back out because his car was too fat. We went out nose-to-nose until I got to the parking lot. Then I walked over and got my driver's license.

I now have a bumper sticker that reads, "If you don't like the way I drive, get off the sidewalk." And I promise I haven't been on a sidewalk since.

VERSED IN VICTORY

Each of the cities in Canaan was a separate entity with different kings and governments. Because they didn't get along with one another, the cities were surrounded by walls. Jericho had a great security system. Those spies no sooner got into town than it was reported to the king, who then sent his own spies to Rahab.

Drawing our attention to Rahab, there are a number of significant aspects that are worthy of our study. First of all, why do you suppose Rahab was willing to risk her life by hiding these men on her roof? Had the king known she was hiding them, he would have put her to death! How was she also able to make the declaration of faith we find in the eleventh verse of Joshua?

> *"And as soon as we heard these things, our hearts melted;*
> *neither did there remain any more courage in anyone*
> *because of you, for the LORD your God, He is God in*
> *heaven above and on earth beneath."*

She knew about this God who had done great works, even with her limited understanding of faith. She knew He was the God of the universe. And because she knew, she was willing to risk her life for a new truth. History tells us Jericho was one of the most unbelievably wicked cities, filled with people who would feed their children to the gods, throw them into rivers, murder them in sacrifices, and commit adultery and fornication. Yet they had the same information as Rahab. Rahab said they all knew about how God had dried up the Red Sea. Everybody in town could look across the Jordan River and see two million people waiting there. Everybody knew of God, and only Rahab acted upon her faith.

The truth is witnessed within our own spirit. It's stamped upon the human heart. Yet, even with that knowledge, people will choose to live in blindness and darkness. Rahab chose the light. She made a stand and was willing to risk her life based only on what she knew in her head. For that, God honored her and chose to save her.

CROSSING THE JORDAN

The women in the cloth-making business would go out of town and peel flax from the plants, dry it on their roofs, then weave it into a rope, dye it, and make clothing out of it. They would take a rope of flax, dip it into a carved-out rock that contained smashed berries, and dye the whole rope. Then, when they wanted to dye another piece of cloth, they would snip off a piece of that rope, drop it into some water, which would color it, and then put the cloth in the water.

Every time we read about Rahab, her title is included: "Rahab, the Harlot." How did Rahab have time to go out, get flax, and cover the roof of her home if she was engaged in the business of harlotry? The rope, which was later used as a symbol, was already colored red. She had already woven together a scarlet rope strong enough and long enough to drop these men down the outside of her wall. How did she have time for all of that if she didn't change professions in anticipation of her salvation?

She must have had over 30 feet of this rope. She also must have had a thriving cloth business. In anticipation of a power she did not yet know and a lifestyle she didn't yet understand, she sensed the life she was living wasn't pleasing to God and she changed in preparation for her future cleansing.

SEARCHING THE HORIZON

1. How did these familiar Bible characters change their lives to live for God?

James and his brother John (Matt. 4:21)

They left their family & their livelyhood to follow Christ.

Zacchaeus (Luke 19:1–10)

He had great faith & expressed it with his works.

_____

_____

_____

2. Are there parts of your life you could change to live more for God? What are some things you can do to live a life more pleasing to God?

be more obedient;   read the word more;

give more of my time & money to God's work

Share my faith w/ others more often

pray more

_____

_____

_____

_____

_____

VERSED IN VICTORY

After the spies returned home, God revealed His plan—the walls of Jericho would crumble, and they would march in and take the city. When the walls crumbled, biblical and secular history tell us there was one portion of the wall that did not crumble. Archaeologists don't understand it, but Christians do. When God gave the order to shout and the walls came crumbling down, every piece of stone and mortar fell to the ground except for Rahab's part of the wall—a part of the wall where a scarlet cord was hung. This was God's provision for one woman.

What we learn about Rahab is you can't fall too low or commit a sin too bad that God will turn from you and no longer make provisions for you. Rahab was a harlot. God knew her history, but that didn't stop God from providing for her.

CROSSING THE JORDAN

I haven't had the direct revelation the children of Israel had, but I know more about God than Rahab knew. And yet, when things don't go my way, I wonder, *Is God really there? Does He really hear my prayer?*

Does He really know about individuals? I bet He knows about other people, but I'm not positive He remembers me.

I think Christians know there is no sin God won't forgive. But there's a lurking suspicion that when it comes to us as individuals, God will perhaps not forgive us of our wrongdoing. Maybe this is a source of trouble to you, and suspicion still lurks in your head— "I don't think there's any victory possible for me." God knows you, He sees you in the crowd, and He makes provisions for individuals. Remember that <u>God sent Jesus to die for individuals, not just for the masses</u>. <u>God is not put off by your sin.</u> <u>He's only put off by your lack of confession of that sin</u>.

SEARCHING THE HORIZON

1. 1 John 1:8–10 contains very wise words about confessing our sins. According to these verses, what happens if we say we *haven't* sinned?

we deceive ourselves + the truth is not in us, plus we make God out to be a lair.

2. What does Psalm 103:12 teach us about God's forgiveness? How does this make you feel? Relieved? Unworthy? Explain.

He truely forgives us, He actually forgets it & does not hold it against us. I am not worthy of His love or forgiveness, after all I put Him on the cross, but by Grace I am saved through faith. And thankfully He is faithful to forgive my sins & cleanse me from my unrighteousness.

A TIME TO PRAY

Heavenly Father, with as much as I think I know about You, there are times of utter darkness in my life. I don't have all the answers, and sometimes my faith is weak. But I learned something from Rahab—that my belief in You can save me. You are the God of promises and salvation. When the mortar and stone fall around me, I'll be strong in You. Thank You, Lord. Amen.

CHAPTER 5

GRACE AND SALVATION

In John 4, Jesus told His disciples they were going into Samaria because there was a woman to whom He wanted to speak. The Jews had nothing to do with the Samaritans because they had intermarried with their captors and were half-breeds. Samaritans also had to wear a distinguishing ribbon on their clothing so the Jews wouldn't contaminate themselves by mingling with them. Talk about racial discrimination! When Jesus told the disciples He was going into Samaria, they were appalled.

Once in Samaria, the disciples went to get some food in a neighboring town, and Jesus went to the well and sat down to wait for one fallen woman. When she came to the well, He began a conversation with her and astounded her by reciting her life's story. He told her, "I've got water for you, and if you drink it, you'll never thirst again. You will not need all these men in your life that have so characterized your adult existence." She went into town and told everyone, "You've got to see this man! He told me everything I've ever done."

As a mental health worker, I have been so grieved in my spirit as I talked with women experiencing divorce, or other kinds of so-called "no-no's" in the Christian world. They have been exempt in service from their churches because of their "mistakes." I'm not slurring churches or church policies. I am saying if Jesus sat on more of our church boards, we'd have more women involved who finally get to talk to others about the pain of divorce. Jesus died for sin. God remembers none of them.

CROSSING THE JORDAN

God is waiting for you at your well. Sometimes we need a good dose of grace to help us remember that we stand spotless before God when we know Jesus. Why did Jesus hang on a cross if it wasn't for every single sin you've ever committed, are committing, or will commit? Otherwise, the cross would have no significance. Not only does God *forgive* your sin, He *forgets* your sin.

When you come to God in prayer, when you gain the courage to come to His throne in confidence, you may hear a little voice reminding you of your transgressions. There's a huge difference in being accused by Satan and being wooed by the Holy Spirit to confession. When we feel convicted, it is very different from feeling condemned. Satan wants to condemn you to a lack of victory, to uselessness, and to fruitlessness. He may have lost the battle for your soul because you've become a believer, but he will try to keep you in defeat by murmuring in your ear, *Who do you think you are, with your history? If people knew what was going on in your life right now, what would they think of you?* I don't think there's a person anywhere that Satan doesn't attack in that manner.

I thank Jesus for my salvation and for His grace. And when Satan starts to bring out my baggage, I say, "Stop! In the name of Jesus, I am cleansed. And by His name and by His act on the Cross, I am free of the accusations that would come to me and rob me of my joy, rob me of my victory, and rob me of my fruitfulness to work in His kingdom until the Lord takes me off this earth."

I hope, as you contemplate what God did for Rahab, you recognize God loves you as an individual. You have the right to feel empowered. Because of His salvation, you are cleansed, and God forgets your sins.

SEARCHING THE HORIZON

1. Read Ephesians 2:8. What does this verse say we are saved through? Have we been saved because of any of our doings?

Grace, no

2. 1 Peter 4:10 refers to grace as a gift we should share with others as it has been shared with us. Check all the ways you help the people around you.

☑ Help strangers in need

☑ Spend quality time with your family every day

☑ Assist elderly people with their bags and groceries

☑ Lend a helping hand and a listening ear to your friends

☐ Open your home to people who need a place to stay

☑ Volunteer as a tutor or mentor

☑ Donate your time to hospitals and nursing homes

☑ <u>Donate to Homeless shelter + help raise funds</u>

If this has given you some ideas on how to share God, that's wonderful! Are there other ways you can share God's grace with others? Write your ideas here.

_____

_____

_____

_____

_____

_____

_____

_____

_____

_____

_____

_____

_____

A TIME TO PRAY

Father, for the joy, for the victory, and for the courage of Your Word, I thank You. For the softness, for the tenderness, and for the reception of my soul, I thank You. I am the woman who has so much trouble taking hold of grace and believing You really have forgotten my sin. Come this very moment and make me aware of Your presence and of my cleansing and inevitable joy that comes when I realize, "I'm okay. I'm guilt free." Lord Jesus, make me a victorious woman that I might feel it and live it and change this world because of it. Thank You again, in Jesus' name. Amen.

CHAPTER 6

REALIZING VICTORY

As a young mother, one of my biggest obstacles was getting my 18-month-old son's pacifier away from him. It wasn't the fact that Jeff was addicted to his little pacifier, but it had gone through such a workout it had begun to smell. Honestly, it was quite rank.

I got him a new one, but he wanted nothing to do with it. I suggested he take it and put it in his mouth, but he spit it right back out and fussed for the old one. I didn't understand it! So I began to study him. He took that old pacifier, put it in his mouth, and it clicked right into place. Then I realized it was a custom fit because his little mouth had formed ridges in the pacifier. It was very comfortable, and to him it felt like home. The new one was smooth. It didn't have any ridges, and it didn't feel or taste like home. His new pacifier had to have ridges.

The big question was, how would ridges form on his new pacifier if he wouldn't suck on it? I determined then, with perseverance and discipline, I could suck on that pacifier and form the ridges myself. I knew it sounded ridiculous, but I really was desperate.

So under the inspiration of that thought, Jeff and I sat down one morning and turned on Captain Kangaroo. He sat down on the couch and plugged in his smelly, old pacifier. I sat down beside him and plugged in my new clean-smelling pacifier. He looked at me, yanked the pacifier out of my mouth, threw it on the floor, and with a very

Are you willing to be taught? Are you willing to wait? Are you willing to trust Him?

emphatic voice he hollered, "No!" So from that moment on, I decided not to share the pacifier-sucking experience with him.

That night, as Ken and I were reading our respective newspapers, he said something that caused me to lower my paper. He looked at my pacifier-stuffed mouth and said, "What on earth are you doing? Are you going to sit around the house at night with that thing in your mouth?"

Obviously, he felt as strongly as Jeff did about the situation, so I said, "No, I guess not."

Then I decided to do it during Jeff's naptime.

I had been working on the pacifier for almost three weeks and was making wonderful progress. One morning I was vacuuming and I thought I heard a knock at the door. Since I was near the door, I held the vacuum hose and opened it. To my horror, a door-to-door salesman was standing there. I kicked off the vacuum cleaner, threw down the hose, and took the pacifier out of my mouth.

Humiliated, I said, "This isn't mine. What I mean by that is, it's my little boy's, and I only suck on it when he's asleep because it bothers him if I suck on it when he's awake, and my husband won't let me suck on it." He held up his hands and burst into the most hilarious laughter I'd ever heard. He laughed so hard he wheezed and coughed and gagged and then started laughing again.

I held up the pacifier and was about to go on with my explanation when he said, "Wait, lady, I don't know what you're doing and I don't care, but you've made my day!" Then he turned and left.

That night when Ken came home, I told him the whole thing and he collapsed in laughter. Then it hit me how stupid and utterly ridiculous it all was.

I had been so into this cause, it overwhelmed me! Two agonizing weeks later, I had finally formed sufficient ridges, and I switched pacifiers with Jeff. I didn't confess the deed to him until many years later.

CROSSING THE JORDAN

The idea of facing an obstacle is probably as common to you and me as breathing. Every day we face some kind of an obstacle. To me, the pacifier seemed like a very real obstacle. I can even say, in all seriousness, it felt like crossing the Jordan River. Is this where you are now in a struggle? Although you've been assured it's God's battle and not yours, you probably still feel deeply responsible. That's because you're human, and we all feel our humanity very deeply.

SEARCHING THE HORIZON

1. We need to recognize that our strength comes from God. Fill in the blanks for 2 Samuel 22:33.

"God is my _____ strength, And He makes my way perfect ."

2. How do you view your personal battle? What is your Jordan River? What do you think it means when you have to wait on this side of the Promised Land? Do you think this battle will make you stronger and more patient? What can you learn from waiting?

weight

_____

_____

_____

_____

_____

_____

_____

_____

_____

_____

_____

VERSED IN VICTORY

Do you remember the miracle of God parting the Jordan River? Most people remember the parting of the Red Sea, but many aren't aware that God did the same thing at the Jordan River. The river was at flood stage and flowed with a very swift current. It was also as wide as a football field is long. Now, that's a rather formidable river to cross!

The children of Israel were looking at Jericho from the other side of the river, thinking, _How are we going to get over there? Are we going to build a bridge?_ Scripture says they sat for three days and stared at the river, not having a clue as to how they would get across it. Even though Joshua was in charge and this was his first big job, he didn't have the answer. God hadn't yet told him how he and the two million people were going to get across the river. Instead, God was asking Joshua and the children of Israel to have faith in His power based on what He had already done for them. He was asking them to remember the miracle-working power that had always been there for them. God was the one who had repeatedly delivered them. He had given them manna. He told Moses to strike the rock so water would gush forth from it. God had already parted the waters of the Red Sea so they could cross safely and escape the Egyptians. He just wanted them to believe in Him.

CROSSING THE JORDAN

You've probably never experienced miracles of this magnitude. However, if you know Christ and you have been living your life with Him as your companion, I know you can pinpoint times when God has been a reality to you and He's come through for you.

He will come through again as you stand on this side of your Jordan. He's asking you to believe in Him based on His Word. He's asking you to believe in Him based on the history of what He's done for you in the past.

SEARCHING THE HORIZON

1. Luke 11:9 should be a familiar verse concerning our prayers. Do you remember singing this verse in a song at a camp or at church? Fill in the blanks to this wonderful verse:

"So I say to you, _____, and it will be _____ to you; _____, and you _____ _____; knock, and it will be _____ to you."

2. As you face your Jordan, think back to the times God met you in your need and came through for you. Share those experiences here.

_____

_____

_____

_____

_____

Prayer Requests

Jim's (Doty) friend's passing

Rick's Dad still sick 7¾

John & Elaina's wedding planning

Ethan's vindication & finding his way.

A TIME TO PRAY

Father, when I look back at all the times I stood on the banks of my problems, looking across to the other side, and thinking, *If only….* I am ashamed by how little I trusted You to come through for me. I have this habit of trying to make the waters part—all by myself. I know it's my human nature, and I can't do what You are able to do. Lord, work on my heart. Help me to trust You with the small things and the big things. Give me the strength and patience to sit quietly and wait on the riverbank until You make the path clear for me. In Jesus' name, Amen.

CHAPTER 7

*J*ESUS THE *S*HEPHERD

When you were a child and nervous about something, you probably said, "Why don't you go first?"

When I was six, my father was a minister in a rural Washington state community. I had a friend named Sharon whose mother and father let her have more freedom than my parents allowed. She was seven, and her younger brother was four. They were allowed to go out to play in the dark after dinner. I wasn't allowed to do that. But when I stayed with Sharon, I would go out after dark and I loved it!

In our community, there was a deserted house. Supposedly, an insane woman had lived there. She was said to have died in the house and had never been buried. Well, you know kids. It was a ripper of a story!

I was new to the area, and I didn't know anything about the house's history. I only knew it looked bad and I had to walk by it on my way to school. Sharon finally told me about the "haunted" house. I was horrified, although I didn't admit it. Since Sharon's parents didn't seem to mind where we went and I wasn't going to be a coward, Sharon, her little brother, Bobby, and I went to the "haunted" house.

As we approached the house, Sharon said, "There's a loose board on the side of the house and you crawl in there and you'll be in the kitchen and then you follow me up the stairs and that's where the old lady's bedroom is and she's lying in her bed."

I said, "Okay. You go first." So, Sharon went first. Then I said to Bobby, "Now you go." And he did.

Then I realized I was outside the house by myself, so I crawled in as fast as I could. I couldn't see a thing. I called for Sharon but heard nothing. I called for Bobby. Again, it was silent. I crawled back through the hole and calmly walked to her house. Sharon and her brother were sitting on their front porch—laughing hysterically.

CROSSING THE JORDAN

As children, when we were nervous we said, "You go first," because we didn't know what lay ahead of us. As an adult, we *feel* "You go first" for the same reason. In many ways, I am still a child on the inside. I am nervous, scared, and insecure in many ways. I find comfort in the image of Jesus the Shepherd, holding me when I don't think I can walk anymore, going ahead of me when I don't feel capable of going first, and holding my hand when I need support. This is an accurate scriptural image of a God who loves me and has provided a Shepherd to lead me. And I know it was Jesus who led the children of Israel, just like it is Jesus who leads us through our own Jordan today.

SEARCHING THE HORIZON

1. Read Isaiah 40:11. Do you think this is an accurate description of Jesus? Describe the image you get when you read this, including the season and the scenery. What do you see and hear? What do you smell? What do you feel?

Jesus is called our shepherd. Summer,
Serene a peaceful. When I think of Jesus, I feel
peace, warmth, love & safety.

2. Do you remember times as a child or as an adult when you said, "You go first," because you were scared or nervous? Share your memories here.

We have all had times when we are scared or nervous about something. But fortunately, by trusting God, He brings a peace that passes all understanding, and gives us the ability to handle all things. Know that we and our circumstances are all part of His perfect plan.

VERSED IN VICTORY

First Corinthians 10:13 reads,

> *"No temptation has overtaken you except such as is*
> *common to man; but God is faithful, who will not allow*
> *you to be tempted beyond what you are able, but with the*
> *temptation will also make the way of escape, that you*
> *may be able to bear it."*

God does not ask us to walk if we're not strong enough. If you are standing on this side of your Jordan and you have no more strength, remember the image of Jesus as your Shepherd. He will reach down and scoop you up like a lamb as He carries you in the crook of His arm. He loves you and He is going to be your Strength. He will not ask you to walk if you can't.

The difficulty we experience comes from thinking God has a different idea of how much we can stand. There have been times when I bargained with God and said, "I think You think I can handle more than I can."

God says, "No. I'm here for you. I'm carrying you and you can take it. I won't give you more than you can take." That is God's Word. We have faith because of what God has done for us in the past, and our burden won't be more than we can handle.

CROSSING THE JORDAN

So why does He have us wait? Why did He have the children of Israel wait? Let me offer some suggestions. God often has us look at our Jordan until we have exhausted all human possibilities. Then He steps in and works His miracle. There is no doubt about Who is responsible because we've completely run out of our own ideas.

Sometimes I get confused and say, "Yes, I'm waiting for God, but what I'm really waiting for is the Jordan to be gone." God has only one interest, and that is our development and our response to Him. The Jordan is no problem for God! It can be taken care of in a minute! But I can't be taken care of in a mere minute because I'm a slow learner. The good news is that God wants even the slow learners to learn to trust and wait on Him.

Examine yourself for a moment. Are you waiting for God to be a reality to you? Are you waiting for God to be a precious Companion to you? Are you waiting for God to teach you? Or are you just waiting for God to get rid of your Jordan?

There's nothing wrong with waiting for God to get rid of your Jordan. However, if that is your *only* concern, you're missing half the point. The other side of the issue is not the crossing of the Jordan. It's the learning that comes with it. It's coming to terms with God. It's knowing He came through for the children of Israel and He'll come through for you now.

SEARCHING THE HORIZON

1. Often we don't rely on the Lord in our trouble until we're tired and think we can't go any longer. Match these verses about trusting God with the correct answers.

<u>c</u> Psalm 107:5, 6   a. Trust in the Lord, lean not on your own understanding

<u>a</u> Proverbs 3:5   b. Whenever I am afraid, I will trust in the Lord

<u>d</u> Jeremiah 17:7   c. Their souls fainted and they cried out to the Lord

<u>e</u> Zephaniah 3:2   d. Blessed are those who trust in the Lord

<u>b</u> Psalm 56:3   e. I can't draw near to God if I don't trust in the Lord

2. Read Psalm 25:5. To what virtue do you think this verse refers? Although you may have learned to use this virtue with your family and friends, do you use it with God?

faith, trust, & love .. Sinc I am human, I am alaays falling short, that is the main reason I constantly need to rely on God. He is always consistant, true to His word, and faithful in His Love for me. He will never leave me or forsake me. And He is faithful & just to forgive me.

God says in Psalm 37:24,

"If he stumbles, he will not fall, because the LORD
holds his hand." (NCV)

A TIME TO PRAY

Lord, thank You for being so faithful. Thank You for not allowing me to be tempted beyond what I am able, and for allowing me a way to escape when it's more than I can bear. Father, I want You to be my precious and constant Companion. I want You to walk beside me. And if it's Your Will for my own Jordan not to dry up and disappear, I know You'll give me the patience to wait and the strength to act when the time comes. Lord, help me to be brave so the next time I'm faced with a big, dark, scary problem, I'll say to You, "Okay. You go first." Amen.

Notes

CHAPTER 8

AN INSPIRATION TO OTHERS

Thirty years ago, at a church where Ken and I attended, I met a wonderful woman who continues to be an inspiration to me today. She was a strikingly beautiful woman with multiple sclerosis—a dreadful disease. She was brought into the church service in a wheelchair, and she was shifted from the wheelchair to the pew. Within a few months, she couldn't be moved to the pew. She stayed in the wheelchair. Within a year, she wasn't coming to church at all. Multiple sclerosis is debilitating, and it paralyzes every vital organ until death occurs— a slow and agonizing death.

Ultimately, this lady was put into a nursing home because she had lost all mobility. She couldn't even scratch her nose. A group of us from the church would visit her with one of our visitation pastors. I didn't get to go very often, but it was always my pleasure, and it raised my spirits when I did. I didn't do a thing for her, but what she did for me was monumental.

One day we had the Lord's Table with her. As we had the elements, we prayed. During the prayer, rather than close my eyes, I looked at her. I had never seen such victory, radiance, strength, and softness than what I saw on her face at that moment. I thought, *Here I am with all my limbs and I can move, and this dear woman is rendered completely helpless, and yet the look on her face is of such peace and joy and worship.* She was my inspiration, my priest.

VERSED IN VICTORY

The ark of the covenant housed the Ten Commandments, which had been given to Moses by God. The ark was about four feet long and two and one-half feet wide, overlaid with gold on the outside, and inlaid with gold on the inside, all according to God's command. The ark of the covenant was held high by the priests, and it preceded the people as they moved across the desert to reach the Promised Land.

Joshua gave the order to the priests at the edge of the Jordan. He said, "Go to the water's edge, put your feet in, and the people will cross to the other side."

Think about the incredible faith it must have taken for these priests to do that! They walked over to the edge of the water, put their feet in, and the minute the water touched the soles of their feet, the water parted. Without flinching, the priests walked into the middle of a now dry riverbed, holding the ark of the covenant, until two million people had crossed to the other side. At that moment, they were standing on the land that was theirs—the Promised Land.

In Psalm 18:32, we learn the source of our strength.

"It is God who arms me with strength, and makes my way perfect."

CROSSING THE JORDAN

Why did God allow this incredible event to take place? I believe it's an example for you and me. Sometimes God does not move until we're on the edge, and by our faith we step into the raging waters. The priests, by faith, put their feet in the water. Peter, by faith, got out of the boat and walked toward Jesus. These were unnatural acts according to nature. But with God, it was no problem at all! Rahab believed in God before she ever understood what her belief meant, and she was delivered from Jericho. Perhaps God is saying to you, "I want you to believe Me, even on the edge of your Jericho, and move ahead without fear."

I would not want to be one of those priests because the idea of standing in the middle of a dry riverbed with water towering on either side scares me. I would think, *What if it all comes down and I'm standing here?* Think of what an inspiration the priests must have been to the children of Israel as they walked across the riverbed. They saw the water looming overhead and thought, *What if the water comes down?* But because the priests were examples of faith and strength, holding the ark of the covenant, the people walked across the Jordan without fear.

God may be asking you to be like one of those priests. Maybe He wants you to be an example to other people by believing and trusting in God's provision. Perhaps your Jordan is a very visible one and people around you see what you're enduring. They might think, *How can she stand that?* And yet, because you are steadfast and have an unfaltering faith in God, you can give strength and inspiration to those who see your plight.

SEARCHING THE HORIZON

1. List at least five people who have been an inspiration to you and explain why.

Dr. Noel Irwin - impressed upon me my need for Christ / salvation

Jesus Christ - my example, my mentor, my Savior

Holy Spirit - my constant companion & consciencous.

Jane - so loving & honest

My Dad - he has been thru so many trials but remained
faithful

2. Do you think you have ever been an inspiration to others? Please describe.

not for me to say

3. Romans 12:9–21 is a powerful compilation of words we should all incorporate into our lives. Write these verses down and then go through each of them, one by one, asking yourself if you really practice them. If there are verses that are a challenge to you, ask God to help you live and love as He does in these verses.

Love; hate evil & cling to good; honor others above yourself; joyful in hope; patient in affliction; faithful in prayer;

_____

_____

_____

_____

_____

_____

_____

_____

_____

A Time to Pray

Father, there are times when I experience a real sense of alienation. I find it very difficult to identify with the miracle of the parting water and the safety of the walk to the other side. I ask You to instill my heart with faith to believe You. Help me believe You are who You say You are and that You love me as much as Your Word says You do. I can only believe the waters will not overtake me when You have empowered me with faith. Enable me to experience a new dimension in my personal faith regarding Your provision and the promises found in Your Word. This moment, bring a precious, sweet comfort to my reality, as I believe in You and give You my Jordan. Give me peace and contentment and assurance. I ask in Jesus' name. Amen.

NOTES

CHAPTER 9

GOD KEEPS HIS PROMISES

While the children of Israel were still waiting to reach the Promised Land, they became rebellious and unpleasant, and returned to idolatry. They tried to forget God. They cursed Him and stopped believing in Him. Yet, these were the people who had the Ten Commandments given directly to them. These were the people to whom God made a direct vow about the Promised Land. These were the people who had the miracle of manna every morning. When they wanted water, Aaron and Moses hit a rock at God's command, and water gushed forth for them. And yet, they dropped their faith like a hot potato because things weren't going well. Still, God kept His promise to them and allowed them to cross the Jordan River. That's one merciful God!

VERSED IN VICTORY

When the children of Israel were safely on the other side of the Jordan, the priests moved out of the riverbed, up to dry shore, and the water filled the river again.

God leads you through your river, which becomes dry and crossable. He doesn't just leave when you're safely on the other side.

God goes ahead of you and He never leaves you alone. He's with you, even when you're safe, and stands in the gap for you. Even after you've reached safety, you may not feel Him, but He's still there. Isn't that a liberating thought? Isaiah 43:2 reads,

> *"When you pass through the waters, I will be with you;*
> *and through the rivers, they shall not overflow you.*
> *When you walk through the fire, you shall not be burned,*
> *nor shall the flame scorch you."*

The waters will not overflow you. As you stand on the bank, you have been promised your Jordan won't be harder than what you can manage. He parted the waters for the children of Israel, but how do you know He will do it for you?

Philippians 1:6 reassures us by saying,

> *"God began doing a good work in you, and I am sure*
> *he will continue it until it is finished when Jesus Christ*
> *comes again."* (NCV)

CROSSING THE JORDAN

God is in the business of perfecting us. In fact, He started a work in you when you first met Him as your Savior, and He will continue

1 Peter 1:6–9:

"In this you greatly rejoice, though now for a little while, if need be, you have been grieved by various trials, that the genuineness of your faith, being much more precious than gold that perishes, though it is tested by fire, may be found to praise, honor, and glory at the revelation of Jesus Christ, whom having not seen you love. Though now you do not see Him, yet believing, you rejoice with joy inexpressible and full of glory, receiving the end of your faith—the salvation of your souls."

that work until the day you die. In His time, little by little, His promise will be realized in your life.

God will not leave you alone on the banks of your Jordan. You may be at a place in your life where God has put something before you that requires courage as well as faith. He knows you, He knows me, and He knows when we're fearful. We can't put on an act with God and hope He won't catch on to our true feelings. He knows.

I learned a lot from the humanity of Joshua as he faced a task that seemed overwhelming. God gives us the same message He gave to Joshua—Don't be afraid, be courageous! Don't tremble, for I will never forsake you.

As you stand on the threshold of having to do something that requires courage and faith, remember these three valuable lessons.

First, what we learn from Joshua is that God understands our human weakness. He understands it and doesn't judge it. Hebrews 4:14–16 reads,

> "Seeing then that we have a great High Priest who has passed through the heavens, Jesus the Son of God, let us hold fast our confession. For we do not have a High Priest who cannot sympathize with our weaknesses, but was in all points tempted as we are, yet without sin. Let us therefore come boldly to the throne of grace, that we may obtain mercy and find grace to help in time of need."

Jesus is our High Priest, our Intercessor to God. He experienced everything you and I experience, so it is He who intercedes with God and pleads our case. Because of that, we are invited to draw close to God in confidence.

Do you know how I approach the throne of grace when I have failed at something or did something I said I would never do again? I mumble. Or I just sort of look down and I don't say much. Scripture says to draw near to the throne of grace with confidence, with boldness, not mumbling or with embarrassment. Why? Because Jesus felt what I feel. I'm bonded with Him, even through my human weakness. For that reason, I can be what He empowers me to be. That's very comforting.

The second lesson from Joshua's response to his overwhelming task is that our security is based upon God's provision. 2 Chronicles 20:6 reads,

> *"O LORD God of our fathers, are You not God in heaven,*
> *and do You not rule over all the kingdoms of the nations,*
> *and in Your hand is there not power and might, so that no*
> *one is able to withstand You?"*

God is a sovereign God. He holds everything in His hands: every government and every ruler. When I read the paper and worry about what's going on in the world, I think to myself, *Relax, God has it all under control.* I might feel as weak as Joshua, but God is the Ruler of the universe, so I can relax.

And finally, the third lesson is this: We are to depend on God's power and not our own. 2 Chronicles 20:15 says,

> *"Do not be afraid nor dismayed because of this great*
> *multitude, for the battle is not yours, but God's."*

Think about that. Take whatever is disturbing you at this moment—maybe it's one of your children, your husband, poor health, whatever battle is yours at this very moment—and remember that God says it's not yours, it's His. And do you know God has never lost a battle? Nope. He always wins.

SEARCHING THE HORIZON

1. What does Deuteronomy 4:39 tell us about God's sovereignty?

Lord is God in heaven & on earth. There is no other

2. 2 Chronicles 20:17 reads,

> *"You will not need to fight in this battle. Position*
> *yourselves, stand still and see the salvation of the LORD,*
> *who is with you."*

Now that you know your battle is God's, can you begin to let go of it? Or are you reluctant? If so, think about this: What can you do that God can't? If you can think of an answer to that question, write it here.

yes

A TIME TO PRAY

Heavenly Father, how I am tempted to try to list all the things I can do that You cannot! My hand is trembling, my pen is poised to pour line after line onto this paper! And yet, You stop my hand. You dry this ink in my pen. You still my heart and my fears. You open me to the truth of the matter. You can do all things. And I can only do all things through Christ Jesus who strengthens me. Without You, Lord, I am lost. Thank you for keeping Your promises. In Jesus' sweet name, Amen.

CHAPTER 10

SEEING WITH THE
EYES OF FAITH

One Sunday morning years ago, I called my friend, Luci, and said, "There's a little church in our community I've been curious to try. Would you be willing to go with me?"

When we arrived at the church, an usher asked us to complete visitor cards. I really planned to attend in anonymity, but I couldn't decline.

As we sat in a pew, I leaned over and whispered to Luci, "I'm going to give them all the wrong information." So, thinking I was incredibly clever, I proceeded to write down my mother's name, address, and phone number in Vancouver, Washington, where I was raised. I handed the card to the waiting usher.

Luci completed her card, and as she handed the card to the usher, I saw that it read, "Mrs. Bernadette Apes." Except it had *my* address and phone number!

The usher handed the cards to the pastor, and the pastor put our cards on the corner of the pulpit with the other visitor cards.

At the conclusion of the service, to my horror, the pastor reached over and took the stack of visitor cards. He said, "We've come to my favorite part of every service when I have the opportunity to introduce our visitors."

He read a name, the person would identify himself or herself, and then he would chat back and forth with that person. Finally, he came to my card and said, "Mrs. Elizabeth Ricker?" This gave me a peculiar feeling because my mother was no longer living. I raised my hand. "Mrs. Ricker, how nice to have you visiting with us! And I see you're from the Pacific Northwest." So, we chatted back and forth about how lovely it is in the Pacific Northwest, and how green and rainy it is.

Then he picked up the next card. "Mrs. Bernadette Apes?" He looked out at the congregation. Luci didn't move. "Mrs. Bernadette Apes? Are you here, Mrs. Apes?" Luci, very shyly, raised her hand. He was relieved.

"Ah! Mrs. Apes. How good to have you here!" Luci said nothing. He tried to work up a conversation with her, but she refused to speak!

He said, "Well, Mrs. Apes, it was lovely to have you here, and we certainly hope you can come visit us again."

Suddenly, she came to life and said, "Thank you. I'm a lonely person."

Well, you can probably guess what happened next.

The following Tuesday night there was a knock at the door. Ken opened the door to a man who said, "Hello, may I please speak with Mrs. Bernadette Apes?"

Ken said, "Pardon me?"

"Mrs. Apes? May I please speak with Mrs. Apes?"

> We can have wonderful intentions and still fail. God has wonderful intentions and never fails. He is always victorious!

"Apes? There are no Apes living here."

After the man left, I explained things to Ken. He thought I should call the pastor and apologize. I felt so bad, so I called the pastor and told him my real name and explained everything. I didn't hear a sound. I began to feel very uncomfortable. Then suddenly, he erupted in wonderful, rich, baritone laughter.

Finally he said, "Marilyn, I cannot tell you how thrilled I am that you called! In all my years of pastoring, I've never come so close to losing it as I did that morning in church."

Apparently, he knew who I was the whole time!

That Christmas, a card arrived addressed to "Mrs. Bernadette Apes." It was signed by this wonderful pastor and his wife, "Still chuckling."

CROSSING THE JORDAN

What a terrific spirit! That's the spirit we need to enjoy the little things, the big things, and the ridiculous things. Think back to the second chapter, when I asked you to visualize your battle in your head, the battle that has been most troublesome for you. Focus on that again and apply these two lessons to it.

First, the battle isn't yours. It's God's, and it's already won. God understands your weaknesses and your overwhelmed feelings. It was Jesus who said in the garden, "If it be possible, let this cup pass from me." Jesus felt fear, weakness, and inadequacy, just as you and I do.

Second, God is a God of individuals. He knows each of us so well, even the hairs on our heads are numbered by Him.

SEARCHING THE HORIZON

1. What does Psalm 31:24 tell us to do when we're feeling overwhelmed?

2. What do you do when you feel overwhelmed? Do you have a hobby or a quiet place you like to go? Do you like to be left alone? What is your earthly comfort? Who is your heavenly Comfort?

_____

_____

_____

_____

_____

_____

VERSED IN VICTORY

Joshua took the children of Israel through the river, and they camped outside Jericho. Joshua looked at the walls of Jericho, but he didn't have a clue how victory would be won. God hadn't informed him yet. God doesn't give us long-range plans either. We learn them the moment it's time for us to learn them.

> *"And it came to pass, when Joshua was by Jericho, that*
> *he lifted his eyes and looked, and behold, a Man stood*
> *opposite him with His sword drawn in His hand. And*
> *Joshua went to Him and said to Him, "Are You for us or*
> *for our adversaries?" So He said, "No, but as Commander*
> *of the army of the LORD I have now come." And Joshua*

fell on his face to the earth and worshiped, and said to
Him, "What does my Lord say to His servant?" Then the
Commander of the LORD's army said to Joshua, "Take your
sandal off your foot, for the place where you stand is holy."
And Joshua did so." (Josh. 5:13–15)

When you and I plan our goals and our battles, we have a timeline, a series of steps. With God, there's no issue of time or planning. Things just happen the way He wants them to happen.

"Now Jericho was securely shut up because of the children
of Israel; none went out, and none came in." (Josh. 6:1)

What did Joshua see? Impenetrable walls. Does he see the victory? No way! God didn't say, "Because of your tremendous military prowess, you will get Jericho." No, God said to Joshua, "I have given you Jericho." God made it clear that it is only He who wins, only He who enables, and it is only He who takes the credit. In chapter 6:3, God finally gave Joshua the plan.

"You shall march around the city, all you men of war;
you shall go all around the city once.
This you shall do six days."

Scripture goes on to say Joshua told the others the plan. He told them they were to circle the city once every day for six days, and then they were going to blow the horns. The people were not to say a word. Then at the end of each day, they were to go back to camp and sit. My Bible commentary tells me you could march around that city in about twenty minutes. That's a lot of day left over after marching!

CROSSING THE JORDAN

Think about how this must have felt to the children of Israel. They were ready for this victory. All their history led up to this moment, and they were told to walk around the city without saying a word, without doing a thing, and then go back to camp and sit.

And what did the people inside the city think? Two million people were walking around the city, and the people in the city must have thought, *Weird! Why should we be afraid of them?* Now, if you were one of the children of Israel, wouldn't you be a little embarrassed?

In therapy, we say to people who are very stressed, "See your situation in a positive light. See your situation exactly as you want it to be. See this already done for you. Put it in your mind as an accomplished fact, and it will begin to change how you think." In your own battle, you don't have to do that because God is telling you to see with the eyes of faith. Maybe you've been flapping like an eagle on your patio, and nothing has happened. A gust of wind hasn't lifted you up yet. In your mind's eye of faith, see your battle as an accomplished fact. God says we can do nothing without Him, but instead of looking at that comment disparagingly, we need to say, "Thank God, because I'm not getting anything done anyway!"

SEARCHING THE HORIZON

1. We should be thrilled to know that our battle is God's battle, and it's already won. What assurances are we given in Zephaniah 3:17?

_____

_____

_____

_____

_____

_____

_____

_____

2. Sometimes we have to believe without seeing. What does Hebrews 11:1 say about faith?

_____

_____

_____

_____

_____

_____

_____

_____

_____

_____

3. In John 15:5, what does God compare us to, and what does He say we can do without Him?

_____

_____

A TIME TO PRAY

Lord, I can't hide my weaknesses and faithlessness from You. I'm so thankful You can see all of me as I am, and You love me anyway. Help me see my circumstances with the eyes of faith. Teach me to follow Your lead without question. Even if it seems unreasonable to me and weird to other people, I'll do my best to follow Your commands. Father, increase my faith, expand my assurance, and enlarge my willingness to follow the Shepherd. Thank You for loving me so much that You are always willing to give me another chance. In Jesus' name, Amen.

NOTES

CHAPTER 11

GOD'S CREATIVITY

There were times when I was embarrassed by the way God decided to do things. Nearly forty years ago, the Lord made it very clear to me that I was to start a Bible study in my neighborhood. I was horrified because the women in my neighborhood were a godless group. I suppose that's why God thought I should start a Bible study group! I agreed I would start one, but I didn't want to teach it. I would have it in my home, but I decided I'd bring someone in to teach.

I was active in the Christians Women's Club at the time and had access to wonderful Bible teachers. But again, I got this very strong feeling I was supposed to teach the class. I thought, *These women in my neighborhood will hate me!* Nonetheless, I went around the neighborhood and invited all the ladies to the Bible study. Every single woman came! I'm sure they started out as merely curious, but they really got into it!

Then my daughter, Joni, was born with spina bifida. These dear women, every one of whom accepted Christ as their Savior at some point, prayed in their very uncomplicated and unpolished way for Joni's healing. They didn't know a thing about healing, but they decided it would be a great thing for God to do.

I remember having a private session with God and thinking, *Your credibility with these women is at stake here.* I had a silly notion that I should be subtle, but God knew exactly what was going on in my heart. So I suggested to God that it would be an incredible boom to their faith if they could see this tiny baby healed. Of course, Ken and I would be grateful for that as well.

When Joni died on the fifteenth day of her little life, I was embarrassed. I resented the way God handled the situation. The grief was incredible, of course, but I was also embarrassed because that wasn't the way I wanted God to do it. I thought He lost a little face. But really it was I who lost it because of my perception of how I thought God should do things. Then I had to face these women and try to explain how God does things in His own way.

VERSED IN VICTORY

The people marching around Jericho were embarrassed. They were a proud group of people. They crossed the Jordan River, and it parted like the Red Sea. Then, they were reduced to just walking around a town.

God gave them the victory, but He did it in His time. He did it in His way. And He did it in a very peculiar fashion—in a way that caused these people to lose some of their pride. I find Scripture to be full of the peculiar ways of God. And I do say that reverently.

There were two young women, Gloria and Donna. Gloria was an experienced skier and Donna was not. But Donna anticipated great success with lessons. After a morning of lessons, she and Gloria went to the intermediate slope. Just prior to leaving, Gloria said to Donna, "It would be wise for us to go into the restroom in the lodge before we get on the ski lift."

Take baby Moses, preserved in a tiny boat made of reeds. His mother put him in this boat and sent him down the Nile. The princess found his little boat, and Moses grew to become the liberator of the Jewish people. Who would think to do that?

What about Goliath? He was this huge giant that tyrannized everybody, and no one could seem to get the best of him—except for little David with a rock. That's creative!

God said to Aaron and Moses, "If you want water, hit a rock." Why didn't He just build a stream? At Christmastime, I often think, *Why would the God of the universe send Jesus to be born in a manger?* I would have put Him in the best hotel! I would have brought Him forth with a better image!

CROSSING THE JORDAN

God is concerned with faith, not image. He placed a tiny baby, who became liberator of the entire human race, who died on the Cross for the sins of humanity, in this dirty, little barn. The point is, God doesn't do things like you and I do them. God is probably not going to deal with your Jericho like you want or expect either.

SEARCHING THE HORIZON

1. You might have heard Ecclesiastes 3:1–8 in a song. Circle how many different stages of life are listed.

      24   29   32   35

2. Have you ever had unanswered prayers work out for the best because they *didn't* happen the way you wanted? What happened in those situations?

_____

_____

A TIME TO PRAY

Lord, how wonderful that You are such a creative God! Even when Your plans are completely foreign to me and I can't understand which direction You're taking me, I know faith is what I need. I'm so thankful You're more concerned with my salvation rather than my image. Father, help me to be more open to Your creativity. Give me a little of what Joshua had to have in order to believe in Your unusual commands. Give me the heart that doesn't care what people think of me as long as I am following You. In Jesus' name, Amen.

Donna didn't have to go, but Gloria did. So when Gloria returned, they both got on the chair to the intermediate slopes. As you can imagine, at the top of the slope, Donna began feeling uncomfortable because she realized how far she was from the bottom, and now she needed to go to the bathroom.

She said to Gloria, "I can't believe it. I feel like one of my kids. I need to go to the bathroom."

Gloria was gracious and didn't say, "You idiot, I told you." But she did say, "What do you plan to do about it?"

Donna said, "Take my poles and wait here on the trail. I'll go behind that tree."

It was very awkward for Donna to remove her ski jacket. She was on a slight slope, which didn't seem to be a problem for her. She assumed the position. To her horror, she began to slide forward and pick up speed. Her jacket was left in the snow, her poles were with Gloria, and she was rapidly approaching the trail. She didn't think to snow plow, she just got on the trail.

There was a young man coming from another direction on an adjoining trail, and she crossed his skis, disappearing into the woods. The young man couldn't believe it! As he looked into the distance at the disappearing pink bottom, he veered off his trail, hit a tree, and broke his leg. Donna was completely out of control by that time. She also hit a tree and fell over, severely spraining her ankle.

Gloria witnessed the whole incident and was speechless. She picked up the jacket and poles and headed off in pursuit of Donna, who had disappeared into the woods.

Donna was not seriously hurt, but all she could say was, "Please pull up the bib!" The ski patrol was called to rescue the man who had broken his leg and the woman who had a badly sprained ankle.

Both skiers arrived at the hospital and were in the same examining room of the emergency room. Donna was quiet. First, the doctor went to the man, whose injuries were more severe and said, "What happened to you?"

The young man said, "You won't believe this..."

NOTES

_____

_____

_____

_____

_____

_____

_____

_____

_____

_____

_____

_____

_____

_____

_____

CHAPTER 12

ACCEPTING GOD'S PROVISION WITH HUMILITY

My parents sold their home in Arizona and made arrangements to move into an aided care facility called Covenant Village in San Diego. So my friend, Linda, and I decided to drive my parents to San Diego. My mother, at that stage in her life, was very uncomfortable and was taking painkillers. As she was dozing in the front seat, I thanked God that things were running smoothly. I saw a sign that read, "Last Rest Stop." At the same time, I heard a funny noise under the hood of the car. The noise got louder, I lost power in the steering wheel, and steam began to pour from under the hood of my car.

I headed for the nearest town, which was nothing but a broad expanse of dirt and land. There was a garage ahead, so I pulled in, parked, and left the door open as I ran to see if anybody would come to help us with the car. Even though it was one o'clock in the afternoon, the sign said, "Closed."

Dad noticed a truck and a car behind us. It was a tow truck! The driver was parked on the freeway beside the most disreputable car I had ever seen. It was painted with every color of paint, and every place you could have made a dent in it, there was a dent. The guy in the car *looked* like his car—disheveled and disreputable. The two men were talking and didn't acknowledge me.

Romans 11:18 reminds us of our humility.

"Do not boast against the branches. But if you do boast, remember that you do not support the root, but the root supports you."

Finally, I said, "Excuse me. I own this car down here that is billowing smoke. Is there any place I can go to get it fixed?"

"Nope."

"Are you going to San Diego and would you consider towing me? I have two elderly parents, for whom I'm concerned, and a young woman with me."

He said we had too many people for him to do the job alone, and two of us would have to ride with "Manuel." He pointed to Manuel in his beat-up car. Manuel never looked at me. I agreed, and Tony, the truck driver, drove down to my car to hook it up to his tow truck.

I said, "Dad, you and Linda will ride in the truck. Mom and I will ride with Manuel." The last thing I wanted to do was put my mother in Manuel's car. It was obvious that Manuel slept, ate, and lived in his car. I started to suggest we clear a space for mother, but he was already doing that.

Linda was horrified as well. She said, "We can't go with them! They will kill us!" Linda had been a student of mine, and we had just read a short story by Flannery O'Connor called, "A Good Man is Hard to Find." It's about a deranged man who comes across people having car trouble and shoots them.

I helped my mother get into the front seat of Manuel's car. Then I turned to Linda and told her my plan. "You sit next to Tony. Put my father next to the window. If Tony tries anything, push him out of the truck and drive to San Diego!"

I had eyeballed the back seat and decided I would sit in the center. There was a huge soda bottle back there and I thought, *If he turns off the freeway I'm going to kill him.* And I probably would have, because nobody was going to hurt my mother.

I sat in the backseat with the soda bottle behind my back, and we headed off down the freeway. I took my ring off, put it in my pocket, and moved my credit cards. I thought, *He'll get them, but he'll have to work for them.* We were headed for the first off ramp when he came to a stop.

With an unfocused gesture, he asked, "Do you know where Tony will stop for gas?"

Still clutching the bottle I said, "No." Then Tony passed us with my car in tow, and we followed them down the freeway. Eventually, we all turned into the first gas station.

Mother needed to go to the restroom. We took a long time, and when we got back Manuel was leaning against the car, looking awful but patient. Tony was leaning against the truck. We got in the car, but Manuel didn't start the car until mother was safely buckled in her seat. I was sitting in the backseat thinking, *Lord, what is this? Who are these two? Angels? Worst looking angels I ever saw!* But we made it to San Diego.

When my parents were safely delivered to Covenant Village, I went over to Manuel and said, "Manuel, I cannot thank you enough for what you've done." I took a large bill out of my purse and stuck it in his pocket.

He took it out, handed it back to me, and said, "No, I was coming here anyway."

I dropped it on his lap, turned to Tony, and said, "Tony, how much do I owe you for this tow?" We had traveled at least one hundred miles. I figured he'd charge me $1,000, and it would have been worth it.

He said, "Well, $100."

I said, "Only $100? That's only a dollar a mile!"

"I was coming here anyway."

So I wrote him a check for $100.

CROSSING THE JORDAN

When my car lost power, I needed two things: a tow truck and a passenger car. And there they were waiting for me! Bad looking, but they were waiting for me. As we made that trek to San Diego from Arizona, I knew it was none of my doing. I had nothing to do with that plan. God did it. I certainly wouldn't have done it that way.

You know what I learned from that experience? God does things in His way so no man should boast before God. God does it all for one purpose: to build faith and understanding of Who is in charge.

SEARCHING THE HORIZON

Read each of these verses and write down what they teach us about humility and God's ways.

1. Isaiah 55:8, 9: What is higher than our thoughts?

_____

_____

_____

_____

_____

_____

_____

_____

2. Luke 16:15: When we concentrate on looking good to others, what does God consider?

_____

_____

_____

_____

_____

_____

_____

_____

_____

_____

3. 1 Corinthians 1:27–29: What has God done to make sure no one is more glorious than Him?

_____

_____

_____

_____

_____

_____

_____

_____

_____

_____

VERSED IN VICTORY

The battle of Jericho was no battle. God wasn't concerned with securing the city. He was concerned with the human heart. God longs to bind our hearts with cords of love, to show us who He is, that we might not become so self-sufficient in who we are.

Whatever is going on right now in your world—your Jericho—God will undoubtedly be bringing about change and victory in ways you do not anticipate and in ways you would not have planned. He will stand with you and for you as you gain victory over your Jordan.

A TIME TO PRAY

Lord, as I close this book, I want to thank You for Your miracles, the way You always show up at unexpected times, the way You make heroes of average people, and the way You constantly remind me that things are not what they seem. Thank You for being a teaching, loving, and patient God. In the days that come, I will turn my River Jordan over to You. I'll march fearlessly into the raging waters and wait for Your command. I'll keep a faithful eye on the path You set before me. Thank You for helping me understand that there is no battle too great and no obstacle too difficult to overcome, because I have You. In Jesus' name, Amen!

Notes

STATEMENT OF FAITH

Women of Faith believes...

The Bible to be the inspired, the only infallible, inerrant Word of God.

There is one God, eternally existent in three persons:
Father, Son, and Holy Spirit.
He has revealed Himself in creation, history and Jesus Christ.

God's creation of the world and humankind
with humanity's rebellion and subsequent depravity.

In the person and work of Jesus Christ, including His deity,
His virgin birth, His sinless life, His true humanity, His miracles,

His substitutionary death, His bodily resurrection,
His ascension to heaven, and His personal return in power and glory.

That for salvation of the lost, sinful man, regeneration
by the Holy Spirit is absolutely essential.
Salvation is by grace through faith in Christ as one's Savior.

In the present ministry of the Holy Spirit
by whose indwelling the Christian is enabled
to live a godly life and to grow in the knowledge
of God and Christian obedience.

In the resurrection of both the saved and the lost—the saved unto the
resurrection of life and the lost unto the resurrection of damnation.

In the spiritual unity of believers in the Lord Jesus Christ
and in the importance of church for worship, service and missions.

APPENDIX A: WORD FIND GAME # 1

If you're going to overcome obstacles in your life, you'll need two things: complete faith in God and a sharp mind. The best way to build your faith is to read the Bible. But to sharpen your mind, PLAY GAMES!

```
S  S  H  E  P  H  E  R  D  G  H  A  M
J  L  E  V  I  C  T  O  R  Y  F  K  A
O  N  L  S  A  L  V  A  T  I  O  N  R
R  O  C  P  Y  S  H  L  A  W  B  L  I
D  G  A  F  S  U  E  J  X  S  E  L
A  J  T  L  U  C  I  M  E  Y  L  A  Y
N  O  S  E  H  D  U  Q  R  B  A  R  N
R  S  B  F  B  X  Q  A  I  X  S  S  F
I  H  O  A  Q  C  N  B  C  I  L  I  A
V  U  H  B  V  N  I  Z  H  G  L  J  I
E  A  Z  J  A  H  L  H  O  H  A  F  T
R  C  J  M  L  K  E  D  E  M  W  E  H
B  Y  E  D  A  B  R  A  H  A  M  N  A
```

WORD LIST

Abraham	Jericho	Manna	Salvation
Bible	Jesus	Marilyn	Shepherd
Faith	Jordan River	Obstacle	Victory
God	Joshua	Rahab	Walls
Israel	Luci	Relinquish	

Answers on page 116

Appendix B: Overcomimg Crossword Puzzle

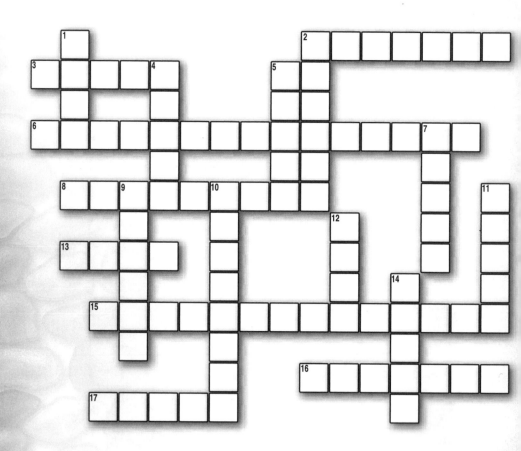

Down

1. Joshua 6:27 "So the Lord was with Joshua, and his _____ spread throughout all the country."
2. Joshua 4:17 "Joshua therefore commanded the priests, saying, 'Come up from the _____.'"
4. The university where Marilyn taught.
5. God provided _____ for the children of Israel to eat while they were in the wilderness.
7. Joshua 3:2 "So it was, after _____ days, that the officers went through the camp."
9. The name of the "angel" who drove Marilyn and her mother to San Diego.
10. While the children of Israel were waiting to enter the Promised Land, they returned to this.
11. Joshua 1:3 "Every place that the sole of your foot will tread upon I have given you as I said to _____."
12. The kind of car Marilyn drove on the sidewalk at her college campus.
14. Seeing with the eyes of _____.

Across

2. Joshua led the people to march around this city before the walls fell.
3. The woman who hid Joshua's men from the king of Jericho.
6. The ark of the covenant housed these.
8. Jesus met this woman at the well in Chapter Five.
13. An eagle needs this in order to take flight.
15. Luci told a pastor in a church she was visiting that her name was _____.
16. 1 Corinthians 15:57 "But thanks be to God, who gives us the _____ through our Lord Jesus Christ."
17. The name of Marilyn's ski instructor in Chapter One.

Answers on page 116

APPENDIX C: WORD FIND GAME # 2

```
H U M I L I T Y E A I S R
B N A N Q U L S B V N Z P
O D R L G V K T W Y S D R
Q E C O A I R X W C P A E
P R O M I S E S B R I Q S
P S D N W F J X E I R L E
H T G G A E O F A Z A J N
S A V I O R I K D U T P C
R N K Y E L C F D E I D E
S D E L A Y E I N G O O E
I I N P H G V Z C A N R K
T N I L A I G A X R F E O
J G U A D C T P N U Q L M
V K A N B L S I J O U A R
Y T I V I T A E R C S X L
```

WORD LIST

Courage	Individuals	Promises	Skiing
Creativity	Inspiration	Rejoice	Understanding
Escape	Plan	Relax	
Humility	Presence	Savior	

Answers on page 116

NOTES

NOTES

NOTES

ANSWERS TO GAMES

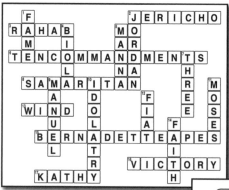

WOMEN OF FAITH

A Division of Thomas Nelson, Inc.

PRESENTS

Irrepressible

HOPE

CONFERENCE 2004

Featured Speakers & Dramatist:

Sheila Walsh

Marilyn Meberg

Luci Swindoll

Patsy Clairmont

Thelma Wells

Nicole Johnson

There is more to life than just staying afloat!
Experience the all-new two day conference that can put fresh wind in your sails — with stirring music, engaging dramatic presentations and refreshing messages.

*We have this hope as an anchor
for the soul, firm and secure.*

— HEBREWS 6:19

2004 Event Cities and Special Guests

Shreveport, LA
February 27-28
CenturyTel Center

Philadelphia, PA - I
March 5-6
Wachovia Spectrum

San Antonio, TX*
March 18-20
AlamoDome

Ft. Wayne, IN
March 26-27
Allen County
War Memorial
Coliseum- Arena

Spokane, WA
April 16-17
Spokane Arena

Cincinnati, OH
April 23-24
US Bank Arena

San Jose, CA
May 7-8
HP Pavilion

Nashville, TN
May 14-15
Gaylord Entertainment
Center

Charleston, SC
May 21-22
N. Charleston Coliseum

Des Moines, IA
June 4-5
Veterans Memorial
Auditorium

Anaheim, CA - I
June 18-19
Arrowhead Pond

Pittsburgh, PA
June 25-26
Mellon Arena

Denver, CO
July 9-10
Pepsi Center

Ft. Lauderdale, FL
July 16-17
Office Depot Center

St. Louis, MO
July 23-24
Savvis Center

Atlanta, GA
July 30-31
Philips Arena

Washington, DC
August 6-7
MCI Center

Buffalo, NY
August 13-14
HSBC Arena

Omaha, NE
August 20-21
Qwest Center Omaha

Dallas, TX
August 27-28
American Airlines Center

Anaheim, CA - II
September 10-11
Arrowhead Pond

Albany, NY
September 17-18
Pepsi Arena

Philadelphia, PA - II
September 24-25
Wachovia Center

Hartford, CT
October 1-2
Hartford Civic Center

Portland, OR
October 8-9
Rose Garden Arena

Orlando, FL
October 15-16
TD Waterhouse Centre

St. Paul, MN
October 22-23
Xcel Energy Center

Charlotte, NC
October 29-30
Charlotte Coliseum

Oklahoma City, OK
November 5-6
Ford Center

Vancouver, BC
November 12-13
GM Place

*Dates and locations
subject to change.*

*** Special National
Conference. Call
1-888-49-FAITH for details.**

For more information call **1-888-49-FAITH** or visit **womenoffaith.com**

The Complete Women of Faith® Study Guide Series

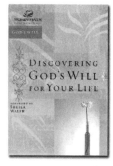

Discovering God's
Will for Your Life
0-7852-4983-4

Living Above
Worry and Stress
0-7852-4986-9

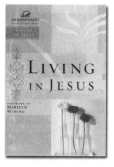

Living in Jesus
0-7852-4985-0

Adventurous
Prayer
0-7852-4984-2

NEW RELEASES

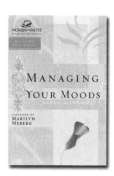

Managing
Your Moods
0-7852-5151-0

Cultivating
Contentment
0-7852-5152-9

Encouraging
One Another
0-7852-5153-7

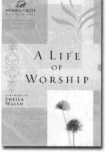

A Life of Worship
0-7852-5154-5

WOMEN OF FAITH®

THE ZIPPERED HEART

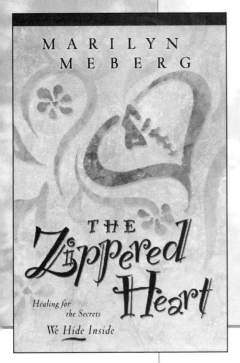

Marilyn Meberg teaches that spiritual and emotional well-being requires us to acknowledge the less-than-attractive, often shameful aspects of our character that we often try to hide. Meberg believes to admit our weakness is to invite the divine power of God to conquer them. With hope and humor, this book is an important reminder that there is nothing God can't heal.

ISBN: 0-8499-3702-7

W PUBLISHING GROUP
A Division of Thomas Nelson Publishers
Since 1798

WOMEN OF FAITH
LIFE STYLE

ALSO AVAILABLE

THE DECISION OF A LIFETIME

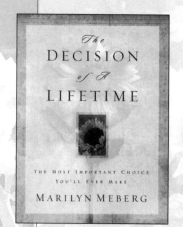

Based on the theme of being chosen by God and adopted into His family, Marilyn draws parallels from her own experience of having a son by birth and a daughter by adoption. In her inviting, delightful fashion, she leads readers to the ultimate question of their own eternal destiny.

ISBN: 0-8499-4420-1

Coming in May 2004
ASSURANCE FOR A LIFETIME

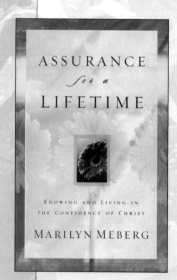

Companion to *The Decision of a Lifetime*, this booklet introduces believers to their new life in Christ. After making the life-changing decision to follow Christ, many new believers are left wondering "What's next?" Written in her warm, conversational style, popular speaker and author Marilyn Meberg explores five topics vital to the health and growth of the new Christian.

ISBN: 0-8499-4500-3

W PUBLISHING GROUP
A Division of Thomas Nelson Publishers
Since 1798